DREAM ALIBIS
JoAnn Stevelos

Artwork by Ryder Cooley

INHALE

    EXHALE

        INHALE

            EXHALE

Not everyone is given access to this other world where the dead and the dying live.
We are not all guests of the dead, this wisest of companies.
If we can't get there by dying, then let's go there by dreaming.

    ~ Helene Cixous, Three Steps on the Ladder of Writing

Artwork by Ryder Cooley
Cover photo by Noah Fowler
Book Design by Mika Dmytrowska

© Dream Alibis 2017 JoAnn Elizabeth Stevelos

Table of Contents

Prologue: Dream Alibis v

Vega, Love 2

Most Days. 3

Walk Along the Edges 5

Widow 11

Lost 12

SpringBeast 13

More Orange 14

Judgment 17

Bells 18

You Are Not Everyone 19

Even 21

Untranslated 22

In Your House 25

Little Red Wagon – One Act Play 27

Epilogue 62

Prologue: DREAM ALIBIS

dream
1: waking life having the characteristics of a dream
2: a state of mind marked by release from reality

alibi
1: an act elsewhere than at the place of commission
2: an excuse intended to avert failure

fragment
1: a broken part of something
2: an incomplete part

inclusion
1: a sense of belonging: feeling respected, valued for who you are; feeling a level of supportive energy and commitment from others so that you can do your best

generosity
1: kindness, especially in giving time to people

maternal
1: synonyms: motherly, protective, caring, nurturing, loving, devoted, affectionate, fond, warm, tender, gentle, kind, kindly, comforting

Section I
POEMS

VEGA, LOVE

Past the crossroads,
I found you cross-legged
hands folded in prayer position
pale and surrendered,
ready to confess:
        You are a Vega in my square
        triangle paired
a dream,
    a root,
        my death.

MOST DAYS

Come as a child to me
Come, climb the willow
Where I built my fort to wait for you
Most days I miss you
Most days you know I do.

WALK ALONG THE EDGES

1
You are a tall oak.

You bring me through the wood,
strides unhurried,
to explore a faraway horizon

We walk through a field
framed in speckled rocks
to lay down among old old pines,
centuries of long exposed bark,
weathered and silent

A tar-blue sky takes our gazes
away from the sun,
and settles them into the thick brush
near a rusted fence
Shivering,
      ascending,
           and eternal,
you sway next to me as we head toward a stone bench
resting on the highest point in the county

I tell you about the baby that is coming soon
I tell you to inhale.

2
Inhale chains of DNA, mitotic division, zygotes
Exhale the biology of what we have done under red pines,
on rough wool blankets grinding into the earth.

Right now, I say,
I need you to walk,
      along the edges,
           and look up.

3
I have to go.
What about the baby?
What about it?
We'll know if it's mine right away.
This is true.
If it's mine, I will do what's right.

4
Today I made my old brother cry.
He called me while he was stuck in a parking lot waiting for
a tow truck to jump start his car.
He wants to throw a reunion party.
All the brothers and sisters will come together,
"Com'on, we'll all be there. We'll lay our swords down at the
door, and just be a family, like the one you always wanted.
What are we gonna do, wait five more years?
Please Sis — Please…"
My brother doesn't know about the baby,
about things that happen in the woods
He stays inside, with remotes and wall-to-wall carpeting,
and bathrooms long overdue for remodeling.
He tries to love me.

5
Outside the garage, I wait unseen by you
I watch your car at the end of the road
frozen at the stop sign.

I take off my clothes,
lay them out on the driveway
and close my eyes.
The headlights glare at my swollen belly.
Car door opens, footsteps on gravel.
You stop in front of me, I will not open my eyes
I will not exhale.
What about doing what is right?
I'm sorry, I just can't.
Please forgive me, please,
you beg as you wrap me in your coat.
You are forgiven, and sent on your way
before my husband arrives home.

6

Even if tomorrow is Sunday
instead of Saturday.
Even if I accepted the idea of parallel universes.
Even if I counted the number of leaves fallen
since you left
It won't make you mine.
"Winter, Fall, Summer," you whispered,
"I'll be back before you know it."
What about Spring?

7

My sister doesn't understand why
I am angry for five years
about some dumb old trees.
Old brother told her to call me
to clear things up before the reunion.
So what, little brother bought our old house
and cut down those trees.

What does that have to do with me?
I tunnel through an explanation,
unearthing tired ghosts.
Big red pines hovered over blue spruces,
and small dogwoods
that needed my tending and watering.

Out to do chores, I would yell
whenever the walls of the house
shook with our stepfather's temper.
Objects, children, animals
— all things to him — things to be thrown around
like broken luggage.

Little brother cut down my safety
and no one thought to tell me.
See you at old brothers.
I threw the phone at the wall,
there was nothing else to say.

8
Atlas,
the suffering one,
is on my mind as I turn down the house.
Slow deep breaths from husband fill the room.
I slide along the wall to the guest bed and dream.
You are taking me and baby
in a canoe across a pond.
I need you to return.
You promised you would.
Don't leave us here.
I mean it — Don't!

Your biceps bulge and contract
as you paddle away to the other side,
your breath
hard and fast
ignoring that your love is my only relief.

9
The baby comes early.
Push honey, push.
Husband is reminding me — push.
Breathe, honey.
Get out. Now! Go!
Husband is confused.
He read the books and went to the class.
Why is she telling me to get out?
Nurse shrugs.
I'll be outside if she wants me.

10
Sweet baby girl.
Look old brother,
look sister,
look little brother.
She is so beautiful.
She's green, says old brother.
She has all her fingers and toes, says sister.
Her name is Red Pine, I say to little brother.

WIDOW (ORPHAN)

The weeping was recognizable,
I've heard it many times,
a broken bond,
the weaker of the two,
left behind.

SPRINGBEAST

The SpringBeast wakes
despite the silver snow
covering the path
as you walk towards me.

LOST

Lost the map of the places we've been,
I'll wait here by the junipers
until you find me again.

Winds blow high, rooms grow small,
You've been gone a long time
Summer, Spring, Winter, Fall.

MORE ORANGE

Among the familiar pines,
far from the City,
I know it's okay to lean towards you.
I inhale. You exhale.
Our arms intertwine and it's okay
that you can't remember anymore
how to get from the rail tracks
to the lovely vista,
just beyond,
up a trail,
through a wood,
where we would see the valley,
and all those possibilities from before.

Our boots break through frozen snow
clinging to battered grass.
"I love the bramble," I declare.
The bramble.
The words hang in the crackling air — real —
like the world we left behind.

We are a lost dream
The flame is more orange than blue
more grey than white.

We stand with the trees,
huddled in our green parkas,
our inescapable past
tangled in the branches.

JUDGMENT

Red leaves covered the ground,
where we stood.

Hands shoved deep in our pockets,
our heads turned away,
from the autumn wind.

The news hung in the air like a noose.

BELLS

The deluge of winter rain keeps me inside,
sifting through old photos,
looking for that one of you and me,
heads together,
eyes alert to the lens that captures
our two grins as wide
as wide as the bells ringing inside me
whenever you come near.

Bells ringing so loud
that I will never believe
you can't hear them too.

YOU ARE NOT EVERYONE

I've been trying to write this sympathy card.
Really.
It sat on my book case in the kitchen, waiting for me
to think of what to say.

It stared at me when I walked by,
and I would swear on the blackest of bibles, that it took a
swipe at me as I passed by and tried to look the other way.

It is an emerald card with pieces of delicate Bangladeshi
grass arranged into a low-lying bush.
I chose it because you like things complicated
— difficult.
And now I must come up with something meaningful to say,
then fold it into its envelope.

I'm sorry to be so direct, and I feel guilty for making this
more tiresome than it should be,
especially when this is about your father dying.

I even thought about using that old standby Browning poem
— "Consolation."

Because it is more important that you hear from me,
than me saying the exact right thing.
But we know this is not true.
Something more needs to happen than sending you
some old Browning poem that I've sent to everyone
who has lost someone.

    You are not everyone.

In the midst of this card crisis I am walking, sitting, driving,
sleeping, and thinking about how I can,
and is it possible,
and is it appropriate,
and most important,
is it meaningful, to tell you that
I miss you terribly,
and that I feel just awful that your father died,
who I never met, yet like.
And I wonder what parts of you look like him.
Your hands, your eyes?

I wish I had gotten to know your dad
and had seen you with him,
maybe out on your big deck,
having a beer together,
talking about the weather.

I wish too that he had seen us when we were happy together
hanging around reading on the big green couch by the
screen door, or wandering up to the loft to nap,
or choosing the best train from Hudson to MOMA.

When I tuck the card into the envelope,
a single blade of grass escapes — swirling, swirling
it lands on this poem.
I fold the poem around the blade,
wedge its pages inside the card,
seal the envelope,
and hear it sigh.

EVEN

Even if tomorrow is Sunday instead of Saturday
Even if we accepted the idea of parallel universes
Even if we counted the number of leaves fallen since you left—

It won't make you mine

"Spring, Summer, Winter, Fall," you whispered,
"I'll be back before you know it."

Don't leave me here.
I mean it.
Don't.

UNTRANSLATED

There is an untranslated region,
 robust when threatened with mutation,
bottlenecked deep in my history.

My trust, loyalty, safety
were stolen by an archaic practice,
blessed by ancient men,
preceding my birth.

Their practices imprinted
on my lungs,
my throat,
my tongue,
attempt to silence
how I breathe my breath
how I feel my heart beat
how I know my truth.

      Inhaling
           Exhaling

Like a red herring
I go about my day.

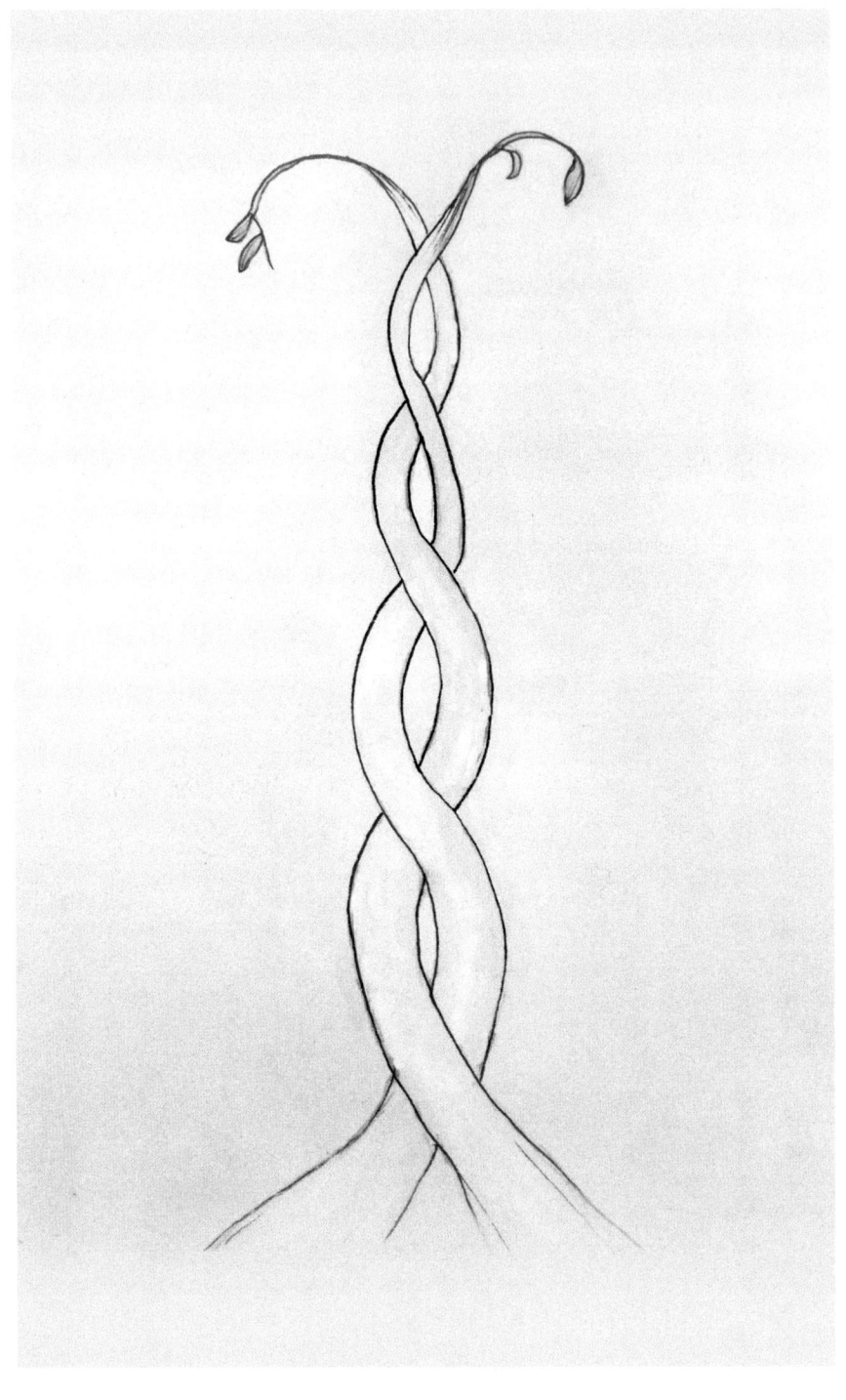

IN YOUR HOUSE

The Barn, a loft up the street from the Old Chadwick
Country Store, had a wooden screen door approached by
a stone pathway littered with roaches of soggy
Bali Shag, and its brass key — always stashed under the
lantern by the carport entrance and warm from the
morning sun — opened everything that was ever real to
me, while the screen door never just closed, but rather
slammed shut, even before I had tossed the key onto the
kitchen counter. In my dreams, I entered your house by
climbing a ladder under the large east-facing windows
above your bed in the loft, where chlorine fumes from the
fiberglass pool wafted in whenever a summer breeze blew
up the hill, past the pines, and over the courtyard.
But now, for real, I am in your house. It still smells like
unfinished sex, expensive Scotch that tastes like peat, and
the woody perfume of the other woman I had discovered
hiding in the corner beneath your new favorite painting,
the one you brought home from Barcelona and posted as
your profile photo on Facebook.

Section II
LITTLE RED WAGON
(A play)

LITTLE RED WAGON
(A Play)

Characters

EZRA: An old guy — like the old guys you find in the West End cafes. He likes being old — he's waited his whole life to be old. He can pull off an old worn out velvet jacket with a rumpled black shirt, trousers, and corduroy slippers. He's intense and self deprecating. He's a poet who appreciates Beat but is more likely to be reading Proust, Goethe, or Aristotle.

WALTER: A middle-aged, solitary person, reflective, struggling. He may be a musician (horn player), or an artist. He is tall, wiry with a goatee.

LUCY: A tall, lanky graceful, young woman with a quietness that feels intelligent and curious. She dresses very modestly, kind of H&M, European cool.

YUMI: A modern, punk, astringent woman in her late thirties. She can pull off black fishnet stockings with shorts. She's the Greek chorus, funny and honest but wry.
She's someone you would see walking around the Castro.

LETTER: In the beginning the letter is in a small envelope that will become a larger envelope each time it is brought on stage. I think of the letter as a character — or as the spirit of Attie.

Place

A big city cafe that feels Old World—like the Hungarian Pastry Shop across from St John's Cathedral in New York City. A place where there is no Wi-Fi, where people come to take a break from their laptop or phone screen and read a book, journal, or chat with people. It's a homey place to be on an overcast, rainy day.

Setting

The stage is divided into three levels. At the center front stage is a small old round café table with three mismatched chairs. A jelly jar of wildflowers sit on the table. A small counter with two bar stools sits behind café table near a door to the left of the stage. Stage right of the café is a set of stairs leading to the second level which is **LUCY'S** bedroom. **LUCY'S** bedroom has a single old brass framed bed. Next to the bed is an end table with a cell phone, lamp, shoebox, books (new titles mixed in with old titles that would have been her mother's—Angela Davis, Helen Caldicott, Denise Levertov, Wallace Stevens, Allen Ginsberg, Noam Chomsky, Hannah Arendt, Ardunhati Roy, Naomi Klein, Chimananda Ngozi Adichie, Ta-Nehisi Coates, Aldous Huxley, David Foster Wallace, Harry Potter) alarm clock, and CDs. Posters of Eliot Smith, Pussy Riot, Ani Difranco, Bikini Kill, Gram Parsons, Diane Arbus, Miles Davis, Wilco, and others line the walls and ceiling. A window over the bed has homemade curtains and rocks hanging from fishing line inside the frame. The shape of a big old Sycamore tree shadows the window. An old Indian print comforter covers the bed. A small worn rug and floor pillow lie beside the bed. Up one level, stage right is an old movie screen; the projector is on the stage floor below.

Notes on Tone

Although this is a serious play, the play is also meant to have humor while being sensitive to the fragile states of each character. Each character is in a different stage of suspended grief. There are also a lot of unspoken moments that can add another level of complexity. For example, there is room for sexual tension to exist between **WALTER** and **YUMI**. There is also room for **EZRA** and **WALTER** to blame each other for Attie's death but love each other too. What should not happen in the play is for anyone to cry. In this play, all the crying has already been done.

The play has two different endings to choose from.
The first ending examines the possibility that Attie's activism caused her to lose hope and die by suicide.
The second ending examines the possibility that Attie died by suicide because of untreated postpartum depression.

(The old movie screen is optional—the play can stand alone without the projection of photos.)

Act One

SCENE I

The lights come up as EZRA *and* WALTER *are talking about the weather.* YUMI *is serving them coffee and staring intently at* WALTER. WALTER *pretends not to notice her.*

EZRA: (Sipping his coffee) Yeah, finally a beautiful day. Shit weather all week. We needed this.

WALTER: (Watching YUMI as she exaggerates washing the counter. She purposefully leans forward so WALTER can see down the front of her shirt.) Yup, finally, sun is out, sky is blue, what else do we need?

(LUCY *enters the café stage left. She has big 80s DJ headphones on and is singing Dust Bowl Faeries "Polar Bear." She hits* YUMI *on the bum as she passes.* YUMI *straightens up and adjusts her shirt.*)

LUCY: "…it split from the shore and we went afloat.
　　　Oh my polar home, oh my polar home
　　　My iceberg melted,
　　　oh oh, my iceberg melted
　　　I swam and I swam but my iceberg melted"

(*Taking off her headphones,* LUCY *sits at the table with* EZRA *and* WALTER)

LUCY: Hey.

(EZRA *nods towards her.*)

WALTER: Hey.

(beat)

LUCY: So why did my mom kill herself?

(beat)

EZRA: Lucy — Lucy, why do you always wait for the most beautiful day to ask us this?

WALTER: Yeah, man — always — the sun is out for the first time in weeks. What's up with that?

EZRA: We'll tell you Luce when you turn twenty — just like we promised — just like the note on your mom's letter told us to.

WALTER: Yeah, when you're twenty.

(beat)

LUCY: I knew you both would forget. (Loudly and annoyed) I'm twenty tomorrow!

EZRA: (Right back at her) Well then ask us tomorrow!

(LUCY *smacks* WALTER *in the back of the head as she stomps off stage.*)

WALTER and EZRA stare hard at each other.

~ Fade Out ~

SCENE II

Next day — LUCY's birthday. Lights come up slowly. EZRA and WALTER are in the same position we left them — sitting at the café table. YUMI is now sweeping the floor. YUMI is ignoring both of them. Wanting another cup of coffee, EZRA keeps gesturing to get YUMI's attention.

EZRA: *(Tapping the letter on the edge of the table)* Well, it's Lucy's birthday.

WALTER: *(Stares at the LETTER)* Yup, it's the day.

EZRA: Twenty.

(beat)

WALTER: Yup twenty.

EZRA: Fuck. Ohhh fuck.

WALTER: Yeah, fuck.

EZRA: *(EZRA begins flipping the LETTER over and under his hands)* That went by really fast.

WALTER: So what are we going to tell her?

EZRA: How about if I start with the late seventies, early eighties and then you take it from there?

(YUMI finally stops sweeping and picks up their cups.)

YUMI: More?

(Both men nod.)

YUMI: Twenty tomorrow, huh?

(Both men nod again.)

YUMI: She wasn't one of those set-yourself-on-fire types, was she?

EZRA: No! Jesus Christ, just bring the coffee.

WALTER: *(whispering)* Offer compassion.

EZRA: Well what am I supposed to say when someone says something that fucking stupid — about her — about our thunder — our hard rain — our Artemis. *(Pause)* My Attie *(Pause)* my daughter. (EZRA *sets the* LETTER *on the table.*)

(YUMI *brings the coffee.* EZRA *and* WALTER *stare her down.*)

YUMI: What's up with the letter?

WALTER: It's a letter from Attie to Lucy. Attie wrote the letter before she left us.

YUMI: So Lucy wants to read the letter?

EZRA: Well she thinks she does but she's twenty. And twenty year olds always think they know what's good for them.

WALTER: Ezra, that's not what's going on. We told her she could read the letter when she was twenty. Maybe if we had talked about Attie more and what happened maybe it wouldn't have come to this.

YUMI: I know it's none of my business, but it's her mother and her letter.

EZRA: You're right Yumi. This is family business.

YUMI: *(Looking at Walter)* Time will tell.

WALTER: Yumi? I can only handle this one thing today, let it go…another time.

EZRA: *(Refocusing after spacing out for a minute)* What? What's happening?

YUMI: Nothing. Just take care of Lucy today.

YUMI *returns to the counter and sits on one of the stool.* YUMI *begins to sketch* EZRA *and* WALTER. *Walter tries to grab the* LETTER *from the table but Ezra gets to the* LETTER *first and puts it in his coat pocket.*

~ Fade Out ~

 LUCY's bedroom. LUCY sits on her bed with her big 80s DJ headphones on looking at photos from an old shoebox. As LUCY looks through the photos they are being projected on to the screen on level 3. LUCY softly sings along to Kyle Esposito and Meg Johnson's "For This World."

LUCY: "Too loud there out on main street, too much to contemplate in my head, only so much can be said, some people made for this world, someone like me, luckiest…"

PHOTO MONTAGE: ATTIE *holding* LUCY *as a baby.* ATTIE *and* WALTER *walking through a field.* ATTIE *and* WALTER *hugging.* ATTIE *and* WALTER *watching* EZRA *on stage reading a poem.* LUCY *as a toddler in a little red wagon.* ATTIE *at a School of America's protest.* ATTIE *and* WALTER *in a wood.* ATTIE *at an Iraq war protest.* ATTIE *graduating from Barnard.* LUCY *as a young girl kissing* ATTIE.

(LUCY's *cell phone rings.*)

LUCY: Hey.

LUCY: No, sorry. Can't. Today is my birthday.

LUCY: Yeah — they said they would tell me — finally.

LUCY: Not sure. Hopefully they will just let me read the letter myself; otherwise, it could take all day the way they tell a story.

LUCY: Summer is a drag here. Occupiers here changed our slogan to "We Are The 99 Percent." It really sucks! "Demand Nothing, Occupy Everything" or even "Corporations Are Not People" are so much more powerful! I am totally dropping out — last night they were trying to get us to sign a paper that said all our actions and speech would be non-violent — after the fucking anarchist arrived! We do all the work and then they show up and try to take over. I'm done. D-O-N-E! This one guy was a total freak and was like trying to show people how to…oh wait *(checks cell- IMs something)* — Oh forget it — doesn't matter — how are things going in Berkeley? *(listens for a minute)* Sounds like the same shit show there. Hey, I gotta get some sleep. Call you later? Love, love.

(LUCY *hangs up the phone, lies back and looks out her window at the shadow of the sycamore tree. Kyle Esposito and Meg Johnson's "For This World." plays as lights go down.)*

~ Fade Out ~

SCENE IV

Café. EZRA *and* WALTER *are continuing their conversation.* YUMI *serves the two men more coffee. She places the cups down in the middle of the table somewhat angrily.* YUMI *grabs her clove cigarettes off the counter.* EZRA *motions for* YUMI *to give him one, which she does, then, even more annoyed* YUMI *heads out the door.*

EZRA: *(Waving the unlit cigarette as he talks)* Twelve years — man twelve tears of trickle-down fuck the poor then fuck them again. Reganonmics, freedom fighting, ketchup is a vegetable, just say no, thousand points of light, star war assholes — twelve years breeding apathy — poor kids didn't have a chance — thought an MBA was the end all be all of their existence on our beautiful planet created — a whole generation of numbskulls — and then there...

WALTER: *(Interrupting)* was the rest of us. Ezra you can't give Lucy this old rant of yours to explain Attie's death. She's too smart for that — and its tired — a tired old way of thinking... you have to tell her the truth and not just the easy part of the truth — the truth that you and I know. We have to get through it first Ezra *(pause)* if we can't make sense of everything together how will Lucy?

(beat)

EZRA: *(Looking over at the door to the café)* I don't want to understand, *(pause - then looking directly at Walter)* and especially with you — because you know that we each think the other is responsible. *(looking back towards the door)* I ain't going there. If we speak your truth — give voice to this long silence — how can Lucy ever love either of us again?

(*holding Walter's hands across the table*) I can't lose Attie and Lucy... (*Ezra stands and begins pacing*). You know she's been going to Washington Square — hanging with the Occupiers.
She's just like Attie. Do you know how scared that makes me! Attie tried so hard to make this world a better place —
it was too much after all her organizing and protesting and marching that a massacre like Tiananmen Square broadcasted across the world meant nothing to the West, didn't even fucking register...

WALTER: (*Defiantly*) ...and the list goes on — the standoffs at The School of Americas, Helen Caldicott's collapse after writing her book "If You Love This Planet", the slaughter of Guatemalans, the beginning of the AIDS crisis, the dumping of the mentally ill into the streets, the first fucking Iraq war, Arab Spring, Tunisia... shit piled up fast — and probably contributed to her depression okay? But it — the depression — was not why she killed herself. And Lucy is not going to kill herself because she stands in Washington Park holding a sign.

EZRA: Goddamn it — yes it was!

WALTER: (*Exasperated*) No it wasn't — it's because we all let Attie down, the world, you, me (*pause*) and death was the only way she could make peace with my rejection and your abandonment.

EZRA: (*Indignant*) My abandonment? My abandonment?

WALTER: Your abandonment Ezra. You left your family. You left her just like I did.

EZRA: No. No. No! You can't make it all that simple, that tidy. I didn't intentionally abandon Attie. It's not like I left her on some street corner to fend for herself. She had her mother —who made it difficult to see her — who used her to hurt me.

WALTER: Bullshit! We both know that you didn't even put up a fight for her. You accepted the situation and saw it as a chance for you to move on. You became the twice-a-year Dad — birthdays and Christmas. You left!

EZRA: *(Sits back down—hands surrendered)* Enough. I was a shit-for-nothing father — (looking towards the door as YUMI returns from her smoke and throws her cigarettes on the counter) but it doesn't change how much I loved her.

WALTER: Yes it did and it does.

(beat)

WALTER: Love requires so much more from us than we ever realize — and if we do finally figure out what someone really needs from us — it's usually too late.

(WALTER *gets up, goes over to the counter and takes one of* YUMI's *cigarettes and goes out to smoke.*)

YUMI: *(Sitting at the table with* EZRA*)* Did you figure it out? What you're going to say?

EZRA: No. (*pause*) Allen Ginsberg said it better than I can. You know, Walter should read Ginsberg. He would get it then. It's all there. Especially why anyone would want to kill themselves.

(*Straightening up — looking at the audience begins to recite a stanza from Ginsberg's "Is About"*)

"The world is about overpopulation…"

(YUMI *interrupts* EZRA)

YUMI: Ezra! Oh god no! Please not Ginsburg! Not Ginsburg again! You always leave out the last lines anyways!

(YUMI *begins to recite the last line*)

YUMI: "What are you about…"

(EZRA *swings around in his chair and stares* YUMI *down.* YUMI *sits down, inhales and exhales loudly, and signals she is ready to listen.*)

(beat)

EZRA: (*Ignoring* YUMI) Attie was out of her mind when she wrote that letter. She'd never want to hurt Lucy — make her choose between us. I don't care what the fucking letter says — it's fucking shit and Walter is a piece of shit for wanting Lucy to read it! He's her father for Christ sakes. He is supposed to protect her — not throw her in front of a train!

(WALTER *hears* EZRA's *last line as he returns from his smoke.*)

WALTER: Ezra, fuck you — see this is why we can't tell her — we can't even work out what really happened and own up to our responsibility. Man — I don't want to fight with you — I love you like my own father but I can't see how any good will come of all this.

EZRA: And it's just that — just that way you give up — give in — that's why Attie is dead.

(beat)

WALTER: Fuck you. (*Exits café door*)

YUMI: Ezra, I agree with Walter. Lucy should hear it all — tell it like it was. It's her mother. We all need to know where we come from or we get really messed up — you know.

EZRA: Do we need to know where we come from? It seems to me most of us spend our time pretending to be from somewhere else.

YUMI: Well then Lucy deserves that too — a chance to pretend like the rest of us — to know where she came from and either accept it, deny it, or use it as an excuse for when she screws up in the world. But leaving her without a story— that's just plain cruel.

(EZRA *looks out towards the audience as* YUMI *gets up and clears the table.*)

YUMI: I'm sorry to interfere, but I love her too (*pause*) she's like a promise.

(EZRA *still looking off toward the audience.*)

EZRA: *(Very quietly, with sincere remorse)* I'm a stupid old man. A dumb bastard — of course we're all fucked and Lucy needs to feel she's one of us — fucked and stranded on this planet just like everyone else. We've kept her world so perfect — so Buddha-like. She probably feels all by herself out there — spinning, spinning, spinning alone — lonely.

(YUMI sits back down at the table with EZRA. She begins to draw him as EZRA turns to sit profile for her.)

~ Fade Out ~

SCENE V

WALTER *is knocking on* LUCY's *door.* LUCY *is inside with her 80s DJ headphones still on. She pulls off one earphone and hears Walter knocking and then puts it back on.* LUCY *is cleaning up her room — changing the sheets etc...*

LUCY: Be out in a sec.

WALTER: Luce, Lucy. I know you're really hoping that we'll tell you everything today — and we will — but not everything. It's too hard. Too hard for your grandfather. Too hard for me. I can share a story that may help make sense of why she died. It probably won't be in the letter though — a lot of it won't — cause things build up and when people love each other, they hurt and forgive each other in unspoken ways. Some people add up the hurts like points and when there are too many points on one side they leave.

(beat)

There are these little deaths that occur in relationships that remind us how vulnerable we are to each other's weaknesses. Sometimes though, we really can forgive each other, we just have to be patient with each other while we learn. I was with another woman when I met your mom — and it was so clear to your mom that we should be together. But I stayed with the other woman. I'd been jumping around in my life too much. I just wanted to get it right with someone — with something — I thought I'd be a better person if I stayed through the hard times — or whatever — I knew it was wrong to stay with the other woman. I should have left and made a life with your mom sooner.

(WALTER *sits down and leans against the door as* LUCY *sits and smokes out her window*)

WALTER: One day I was walking down Main and across the street I see Attie pulling this little red wagon with a baby girl. As she got closer I knew right away you were mine. I walked up to Attie and took you from her. Attie asked me to carry you home. So I did. I couldn't believe I was getting this second chance with your mom. I was about the happiest I have ever been that day — the day I met you and the day I got to love Attie the way I was meant to.

(beat)

But things are never that simple Lucy. Even after we moved in together — it just wasn't the same. Attie always felt that first rejection. She never got over it. As much as I tried to step up she never trusted that I was really there because of her—because of my love for her—she believed that if it wasn't for you I wouldn't have come back to her—that's partly true but I really was thankful for a second chance. I could never make her feel that.

(WALTER *lays down with his arms behind his head as* LUCY *lays down on the bed and checks her cellphone*)

WALTER: Your mom — she used to spiral down — that's how she'd describe it. She didn't like to spend a lot of time alone. She'd get wacky when there was too much silence. It may be why she kept so busy. So she didn't have to figure out who she was.

What she thought about things—how she felt you know, really felt about the decisions or the lack of decisions she'd made in her life. You, me, the whole activist-organizing thing was her way of not having to think about what would have really made her happy. I could never figure out what she wanted from life—needed from life—needed from me.
She always needed someone else to need her for something. It was like she never believed that someone would just love her because she existed. Cause she was Attie. When she got like that I'd try to get her to walk with me. We'd walk up this big hill that went through a wood and then to this overlook where you could see the whole valley. One day, I came home and she was in the middle of a meltdown. I think you were about two. We left you with Ezra to go for a walk. We never said much when we walked. Sometimes at the overlook we'd sit and hold each other.

(beat)

It's just something we did. It's the only way I knew how to ground her so that she could get past it. But you know sometimes I was tired too, tired of trying to reassure her, prove myself to her, make her understand that I just loved her for her. When she got like that, that freaky crazy look in her eye she'd let go of everything and closed me out—it really hurt, deep, like I wasn't good enough for her. I felt like maybe she was right. I couldn't love her the way she needed to be loved—and then I'd get angry, really pissed because I knew it wasn't true. I couldn't understand why she was putting us through this.

(beat)

So we are out on the walk. I tell her that I'm angry that she is doing this to us, that if this wasn't what she needed, then she should go out and find something that was better. She went hysterical. We're in the middle of the wood and she's sobbing and hitting me and I can't figure out how to help her. She could never forgive me—not for the rejection and now not for this. Honestly—I was just tired, tired of trying to help her. I told her she needed to get help from — a counselor — or something because I couldn't keep having this same conversation over and over again. I fucked up so bad. She just needed me to be there for her one more time and I was tired. I wish I hadn't been so tired Lucy. I wish I could change that whole day. That was near the end. *(pause)* I know you want to know everything.

(WALTER *stands up.* LUCY *stands up and heads towards the door.*)

(beat)

WALTER: Attie didn't mean to leave you. She's just punishing me.

(LUCY *still with her headphones opens the door.* WALTER *and* LUCY *are startled by each other.* LUCY *walks by* WALTER *and down the stairs*)

LUCY: Hey

WALTER: Hey.

(WALTER *follows* LUCY *down the stairs as the lights fade out.*)

~ Fade Out ~

SCENE VI

Todd Nelson's "Laugh instead of Cry" is playing. YUMI, humming along, is wiping down the counter. EZRA and WALTER are right back where they started except it is evening now. EZRA is pushing the LETTER around on the table. WALTER reaches for it and EZRA slaps WALTER's hand. EZRA makes a grand gesture of putting the LETTER back in his pocket and heads outside for a smoke.

YUMI: *(Walks over to the table)* So?

WALTER: I have to tell you something.

(YUMI *makes an EZRA-like gesture with her hands for* WALTER *to keep talking.*)

WALTER: It wouldn't be right if I didn't say.

YUMI: Uh huh? *(again with the gesture but more EZRA-like exaggerated.)*

WALTER: I tried to talk to Lucy today but...

YUMI: *(Surprised and upset)* Without me? Jesus Walter. It's like I don't exist or something. I'm too old to be running after you. Either your in or your out. Which is it?

(YUMI *marches over to the wall and rips down all of her drawings. She throws them on the floor and begins stomping on them like a mad woman. She's super pissed from all their unresolved fights.*)

YUMI: Really fucking sick of it! Just keep pushing everyone out of your life. First Attie, now me — keep going and you will lose Lucy too. *(she takes a deep breath and calms down)* I know you hate when I do this but I have to tell you about a dream I had last night...

WALTER: Oh Yumi, please not now, not another dream. I just can't...

YUMI: Let me — I promise it's quick. I dreamed I was dreaming I was an artist working as barista dreaming I was an artist.

WALTER: What? What are you talking about. You are an artist working as a barista!

YUMI: No — that's why I'm telling you — I'm really the barista trying to act like an artist — and that is why you can't love me like you loved Attie — if I was brave enough to be true to myself — like Attie was as an activist — than I'd be an artist working as an artist.

(WALTER *moves toward* YUMI *cautiously. He has seen and heard all this before.*)

(YUMI *turns her back to him.* WALTER *gently puts his hands on her shoulders and hugs her from behind.*)

WALTER: Yumi. Please stop. I do love you. Right now I have to take care of my daughter. Please. Please Yumi?

(WALTER *takes the drawings and tapes them back up on the wall but does a terrible job of it.*)

WALTER: *(Starting again)* I....

YUMI: *(Interrupting again)* Why? So you can be the one she chooses. That's low Walter — and without Ezra too?

WALTER: Let me finish please. *(Yelling this time)* BUT she didn't hear me because she had her headphones on.

And then it occurred to me that I've never asked Ezra if he's read the letter.

YUMI: No, *(hesitating)* I don't think Ezra has read the letter. Have you?

WALTER: No — of course not!

YUMI: Of course not! Why wouldn't you?! She was your wife! Didn't you want to know why?

WALTER: No — I didn't want to know why—its been easier not to. Besides Ezra has kept it under lock and key. He's never wanted to know what Attie was really thinking.

(EZRA *has returned and overhears* WALTER *and* YUMI)

EZRA: No, it doesn't matter what she was thinking! Always been clear to me — quite clear in fact — that she was not thinking! She wasn't herself. My Attie wouldn't have left us, left her daughter. She loved Lucy. It just doesn't make sense that she would leave her — leave us.
So, therefore, it can't be her who did this. It was not my Attie who killed herself. It was someone else — someone I don't know. Someone that took her over — that pushed out all of who she was — all that was good and strong inside her. It happens you know — people lose themselves.
That's what families are for. To help them remember who they are — and that was what I was supposed to do — help her find herself again — help her hold onto herself — to my little girl Attie who always wanted me to hold her up high in the air so she could touch the sky — to my angry teen who hid in her room making chapbooks and zines —

hold onto my sweet Attie who thought it was funny to hide my cigarettes — or who wouldn't talk to me for a year after I split from her mother.

(LUCY *comes walking in with her headphones still on singing Dust Bowl Faeries, "Polar Bear".*)

LUCY: "Well now I'm the star of the North Pole Show
　　　　The icebergs are plastic and there is no more snow
　　　　They tell me the pole has seen better days
　　　　The ice has all melted and the fish swam away…"

WALTER: Hey.

LUCY: Hey.

(LUCY *Stares at the* LETTER *on the table.* EZRA *and* WALTER *look at each other—daring each other.*)

YUMI: Can I get you something Luce?

(*All three turn to glare at* YUMI. YUMI *walks away mumbling about what jerks they all are.*)

LUCY: (*Starting again*) Well? Are you gonna give me the letter?

EZRA: Here's what I'm thinking. We have this letter (*pushes it around the table*) and you're twenty today. And we have our instructions from Attie to give you this letter. But before we go ahead—I want us to think this through together. Attie wouldn't mind too much because she was always mad at me for not listening to her anyway.

(EZRA *makes a grand gesture of reaching into the inside pocket of his tweed coat and pulls a folded piece of yellow legal paper that has a handwritten list.*)

EZRA: I have made a list of possibilities. One. Walter and I tell Lucy why we think Attie died and then Lucy reads the letter. Two. Lucy reads the letter first and then we tell Lucy why we think Attie died. And three. Lucy does not read the letter (EZRA *peeks over the list at Lucy to see her reaction*) — cause it doesn't really matter what the letter says — we love you and loved Attie.

(*The three sit looking at the LETTER. YUMI sits looking at the three as she draws. LUCY stands up, takes the LETTER from EZRA's hand, folds the list around it and then puts them both in WALTER's coat pocket.*
LUCY *puts her headphones back on and walks off stage half humming-half singing Bob Dylan's "Little Red Wagon"*)

LUCY: "Little red wagon — hmmm — ain't no monkey...

(*The song plays out as more of the shoe box photos are shown on the projector.*)

~ Fade Out ~

NOTE: This play has two possible endings, therefore there are two SCENE VIIs.

Ending One

SCENE VII

YUMI *straightens the portraits on the wall behind the counter.* WALTER *has made a mess.* WALTER *rests his head on the table.* YUMI *looks over and tenderly kisses the portrait of* WALTER *then goes over and half hugs him and kisses him on the head.* WALTER *sits up and reaches into his pocket and takes out the* LETTER. WALTER *unwraps the list from the* LETTER *and sets it aside. He leans the* LETTER *against the jelly jar of flowers and stares at* IT. YUMI *sits down and touches the* LETTER. WALTER *does not respond.* YUMI *slides the* LETTER *towards her.* WALTER *still just stares at the* LETTER. YUMI *picks up the* LETTER, *looks at* WALTER *one last time for permission.* WALTER *says nothing and this time looks away.* YUMI *opens the* LETTER *and hands it to* WALTER. WALTER *hesitates. Scared, he begins to read the* LETTER. *He doesn't notice that* LUCY *has returned.* LUCY *sees* WALTER, *takes off her headphones and listens. Walter begins to read* ATTIE'S LETTER.

WALTER: Dear Lucy,

LUCY: (*Charging at* WALTER *to stop him from reading further*) STOP! That's mine. How could you? How could you both? She's my mother, my mother, not yours! Give that to me.

(LUCY *grabs the letter, rips it up into little pieces, and throws it in the air, as* EZRA *reenters the cafe —* EZRA *stops frozen.* LUCY *is frozen in place looking shocked by what she just did. Everyone is frozen. Lights go down and then come back up.*)

(Beat)

(YUMI, WALTER, EZRA *and* LUCY *all break out of their frozen states at the same time and begin to scurry around the stage picking up pieces of the letter and reading them aloud to the audience. It is a fury of activity, sometimes the actors speaking over each other shouting out their lines, other times quietly saying their lines, and other times reading the paper first reacting and then reading it aloud. The actors will have the following lines set for them but as they are picking up the pieces of the letter they should feel free to improvise if a section they pick up off the floor supports the rhythm.*)

WALTER: …something I can't explain to anybody, not Ezra, not Walter…

YUMI: …I am looking at the world from a deep black hole… my little koan…

WALTER: …I tried to make this world a better place for you…

EZRA: …dear lucy, my sweet fawn, my… please forgive me…

YUMI: …always know that I love you…

LUCY: …love this world…I am tired…

WALTER: …be strong, fight with everything…

LUCY: …be courageous and brave…

YUMI: …I imagine you strong and beautiful and intelligent…

EZRA: (sits down without a piece of the letter and simply repeats Yumi's last lines—he is tired) …strong and beautiful and intelligent…

~ THE REAL LETTER ~

My dear sweet Lucy,

If you are reading this letter, then you must be twenty.
A young woman who I wish, with all my heart, feels how deeply I loved her.

My sweet girl, a void, blacker than black surrounds me and all I can do is retreat to a small place inside where I fight until I am numb. I am tired. Nothing I have done has helped make this world a better place for you. Nothing I have done has stopped the tsunami of hate and greed that swells up and drowns all that is good and kind and just. I am frightened of this world for you and I can't watch it harm you—my innocent—my vulnerable sweet girl. My heart is broken and I can't watch the world break yours. I can't explain this darkness to anybody, not Ezra, not Walter. I don't understand how could the most profound thing that has ever happened to me, giving birth to you, makes me so sad?

Please listen to me when I say, live your life with courage but know when to give in and take care of yourself before you get too tired. Bearing witness to despair and injustice is a duty but it is not all that you are born to do. I wish I knew this sooner. I hope that the world has become a better place for you. I don't want you to suffer as I am now. It's as if I am looking at myself from a deep black hole, and you, so happy, and so beautiful, are spinning far from my reach. It is so painful to watch you grow from this distant sad place when you need so much more from me with each new day.

I can't bear how much I have failed as your mother and as someone who wanted so much to bring peace and love to your world. There was always so much to be done. I need you to understand that my having to end things now has nothing to do with how much I love you. My only hope is that you will not hate me and that one day you will be able to forgive me.

I love you, and I am sorry. Be strong. Please forgive me.

~ The End ~

NOTE: *No one has recorded the number of activists that have died by suicide. People, like my character Attie, leave behind complex public and personal stories that collide with our deep desire for hope and our shared reality of the increasing possibility that global warming, water depletion, disease pandemics, racial and social injustices, economic instability, and social upheaval will create a nightmare future for us in the 99 percent.*

Our shared humanity must be the foundation from which we demand justice and peace for all living things on this beautiful and mysterious planet.

This ending is in honor of MurShawn M. McCarrel II, a leading member of the state's Black Lives Matter movement who died by suicide on the steps of the Ohio statehouse on February 8, 2016.

Ending Two

SCENE VII

WALTER, LUCY and YUMI *are all dressed in funeral clothes.* WALTER *is sitting at the café table. He stares at the chair EZRA sat in.* YUMI *has her sketches of EZRA taped to the wall behind the counter.* LUCY *with her big 80s DJ head phones on, walks in, stops in front of* YUMI *and leans into her.* YUMI *(visibly pregnant with* WALTER's *child) is busy making coffee.* WALTER *stands and takes off* LUCY's *headphones and lays them on the table in front of her.* WALTER *sits down and reaches into his pocket. He takes out the* LETTER *with* EZRA's *list still wrapped around it. He puts the* LETTER *next to the headphones.*

WALTER: This belongs to you now.

(WALTER *stands, walks around to the back of* LUCY's *chair, hugs and kisses her tenderly, then walks out the door.* YUMI *purposefully does not watch him leave, instead she watches* LUCY.)

(beat)

(LUCY *stands, picks up the headphones and begins to put them on but instead puts them on the back of* EZRA's *chair.* LUCY *walks over to the counter, sits on the stool next to* YUMI *and hands her the* LETTER.)

YUMI: Lucy, I know it doesn't feel like it now—but things will get better—be better...

(LUCY *rests her head on the counter and shakes her head back and forth. Her whole body rejects what* YUMI *is saying.*)

YUMI: Ezra loved you very much. Your mother loved you very much. I wish I knew how to stop your heart from breaking...

(YUMI *takes* LUCY's *face in her hands, kisses her gently on the bridge of her nose looks at her intently—inhales and exhales— as if to give* LUCY *strength.* YUMI *sets the list aside and opens the* LETTER. LUCY *tears up but doesn't cry.* YUMI *scans the* LETTER *then looks to the audience with despair.* YUMI *stumbles and hesitates as she begins to read.*)

YUMI: Dearest Lucy, my favorite person on the planet, my little koan, my sweet fawn, my love. You must be twenty since you are reading this letter, a woman, a lovely young woman full of hope and promise. I imagine you strong and beautiful and intelligent — really fucking intelligent...

(YUMI *continues to read as "Crestfallen" by Todd Nelson plays over her so the audience can't hear anymore. The real* LETTER *is up on the projector so that the audience can see that Yumi is making it up as she goes along.*)

~ THE REAL LETTER ~

My dear sweet Lucy,

If you are reading this letter, then you must be twenty. A young woman who I wish with all my heart, feels how deeply I loved her.

My sweet girl, I don't know what is happening to me and I don't know how to stop this darkness—this demon that has entered my soul. I don't know who I am anymore. A void, blacker than black surrounds me and all I can do is retreat to a small place inside where I fight until I am numb. I am frightened by the thoughts that remain constant since you were born. I am afraid I may harm you and that feeling brings me such unbearable distress. Something terrible has happened to me since I gave birth to you. Something I can't explain to anybody, not Ezra, not Walter. I don't understand how could the most profound thing that has ever happened to me makes me so sad?

Please listen to me when I say do not have a child. I am not sure if this terrible fate could be passed to you but I don't want you to suffer as I am now. It's as if I am looking at myself from a deep black hole. And you, so happy, and so beautiful, are spinning far from my reach. It is so painful to watch from this distant sad place when you need so much more from me each day. I can't bear how much I have failed as your mother. I need you to understand that my having to stop this dreadful pain has nothing to do with how much I love you.

My only hope is that you will not hate me and one day that you will be able to forgive me for this.

I love you, and I am sorry. Be strong. Please forgive me.

~ The End ~

NOTE: *One in seven women have depression in the year after they give birth according to a JAMA study released on March 13, 2014.*

Suicide is the second leading cause of death in postpartum women. This ending is in honor of all the women who have died from suicide from untreated postpartum depression.

Epilogue

Truth, art, and fiction collide when a dream, an alibi, and a fragment are connected into a work that we may not have felt free to express otherwise.

Made in the USA
Middletown, DE
18 September 2020